CW01665460

Evie & the Farm

Evie's Secret Hiding Place

Other titles in the Evie & the Farm series
Evie's Afraid of the Dark
Evie to the Rescue
Evie's Spiky Friend
Evie's Christmas Plan

First published in 2023 by Stag & Robin Publishing
Text copyright © Mia George
Illustrations copyright © Mia George

All rights reserved. No part of this book may be reproduced, transmitted or stored in an information retrieval system in any forms or by any means, graphic, electronic or mechanical, including photocopying, taping and recording without prior written permission from the publisher.

ISBN 978-1-7393812-2-6

Evie doesn't live on a farm, or even in the countryside. She lives in a big, hustling and bustling city. Every school holiday, she travels with her Mum, Dad, and older sister, Marie, to go to see her cousins who live far away on a farm. Evie doesn't mind the 5-hour train journey one bit.

As she looks out the train window, leaving the bright lights and tall buildings of the city behind, she wonders what adventure awaits her next...

To Dad, a man of few words and who was therefore the best secret keeper.

Inspired by fond memories at Muirhouse Farm

Evie & the Farm

Evie's Secret Hiding Place

A Story by Mia George

Evie's favourite activity on the farm was exploring. She was told she mustn't venture past the front gate onto the road, or past the cow shed where all the machinery and tractors were kept. But Evie didn't mind; she felt there were enough things to see and do on the farm.

She could hide amongst the tall reeds in the garden,

sit nestled between large bales of hay,

wander through the large sheep barn,

and feed the chicken in their coops.

Evie spent hours at a time playing in and around the farm, and she always came home very dirty indeed. Mum said she must surely spend most of her holiday washing Evie's clothes, scrubbing her boots, and attempting to wash mud out of her hair.

But Evie wasn't bothered about a bit of muck. As soon as she was clean, she was off, ready for her next adventure!

The best thing about exploring was that Evie knew all the hiding places. So that was why, when Evie's sister Marie suggested playing hide-and-seek one warm summer's day, Evie could barely contain her excitement.

As they couldn't decide who amongst them should be seeker, her cousin, Christopher, suggested asking one of the parents. Auntie Anne was at work that day, so they asked Mum.

“Sounds like a great idea,” said Mum, as she put down her book and stood up. “I’m going to count to one hundred, starting from… NOW!”

Mum walked quickly to the corner of the garden and turned around so that she couldn’t see where they were going. Covering her eyes, she began counting loudly, “One... Two... Three...”

Meanwhile, Evie, Marie, Christopher, and Evie’s other cousin, Alistair, scrambled, running this way and that, trying to find a place to hide.

Evie was out in the lead, heading straight to the large rowan tree near the garden entrance.

The tree was very old, and had a great thick trunk. Its many long branches, cloaked in the green leafy sleeves of summer, spread wide to her left and right as she approached, almost inviting her to bury herself in amongst them.

Yet as she planted her right foot on the lowest branch and looked up to plot her route upwards and inwards, Alistair arrived at the base of the tree. Without any hesitation, he clambered up past her.

"Snoozers are losers!" Alistair teased, already making it to the third branch up. "This is my hiding place now; you'd better find somewhere else."

Evie climbed back down from the branch, surprised and annoyed. But there was no time to argue; she could loudly hear her Mum chanting, "Twenty-seven... Twenty-eight... Twenty-nine..."

Shaking off her disappointment, she decided on the next best hiding place: the coal shed. It was somewhere she usually avoided - the darkness that lay behind its cracked windows made her feel uneasy. Mum's counting still echoing in her ears, she reassured herself that if she couldn't see in there, then she couldn't be seen either. Gathering her courage, Evie slowly opened the creaky coal shed door and peered inside.

But there was already someone there!

"I'm hiding here!" Marie said, turning her nose up and standing in a way so that she didn't touch the coal that was arranged in piles on the floor, or the dirty, sooty walls. "And anyway, it's much too *scary* for you in here."

Evie sighed, but felt secretly relieved all the same. She was, though, getting desperate now.

"Fifty-four… Fifty-five…"

Where else could she hide?

The bale barn! She strode quickly from the coal shed, past the gate, and round to the side of the courtyard. Carefully avoiding the stretch opposite that contained the machinery, she entered the bale barn.

The bale barn stored many, many bales of hay. They were all packed tightly into black bags, round like Swiss rolls, and stacked one on top of the other in long lines. Evie liked it in here. It was very quiet, and the air had a strong, sweet scent.

She was just wondering how best to conceal herself when she noticed a pair of feet sticking out from the top of a hay bale.

“Evie! Come join me up here, it’s a great place to hide,” Christopher called down kindly in a hushed voice.

But Evie wasn’t used to climbing that high up on the bales. She tried a couple of times but lost her footing on the glossy black bag and tumbled back.

“Ach, never mind,” Christopher said. “Although you better quickly find someplace else, we don’t have long left!”

Evie felt frustrated. Why was this proving to be so difficult?

She made her way out of the bale barn and stopped to have a good think.

From the garden, she could faintly hear, "Eighty-one… Eighty-two… Eighty-three…"

Evie suddenly had a burst of inspiration. She couldn't believe she hadn't thought of it before.

Running now, Evie made her way back to the garden. She sneaked behind her Mum's turned back over to the hedge on the far side.

Crouching down to her knees, she crawled through a narrow parting in the hedge, amidst spiky branches and rough leaves. They snagged at her clothes, but with careful effort, she made it through without a scratch.

Evie found her usual small space on the dirt floor and turned to sit cross-legged on her bottom. She looked around at the leafy dome, held up by a web of branches of all sizes. The sun filtered through the hedge, making the leaves glisten and sparkle, but she was quite sure she was invisible from the outside. To one side, Evie heard the steady hum of bees encircling a neighbouring flower bush, while the breeze that rippled through the garden reeds sent a cascading whistle to the other. Evie breathed in the earthy air, leaned back, and waited.

“Ninety-eight… Ninety-nine… ONE HUNDRED! Here I come, ready or not!” Mum finished.

Evie listened as Alistair and Marie were found in turn, each then joining Mum on the search.

She heard their feet crunching across the pebbly courtyard,

and wading through the swishy garden grass.

“Evie, Chris, where are youuu?” Marie sang.

But Evie knew better than to give away her hiding place, when she was so close to winning.

Finally, she heard a distant “Ah-ha, I see you up there!” Mum had found Christopher!

When she was sure that Christopher had joined in on the search, and they were well away from her own hiding place, Evie crept back out of her little nest. Her Dad, who alone had seen where she had gone to hide, smiled at Evie and tapped his nose.

Evie skipped back into the courtyard and saw the backs of her Mum, sister and cousins in the cow shed.

"Here I am!" Evie pronounced triumphantly. "I WIN!"

Evie's leafy den remained secret to everyone (besides Dad, of course). Evie preferred it that way. It was her very own hidey-hole – strictly for little people!

The Evie & the Farm Series Collection

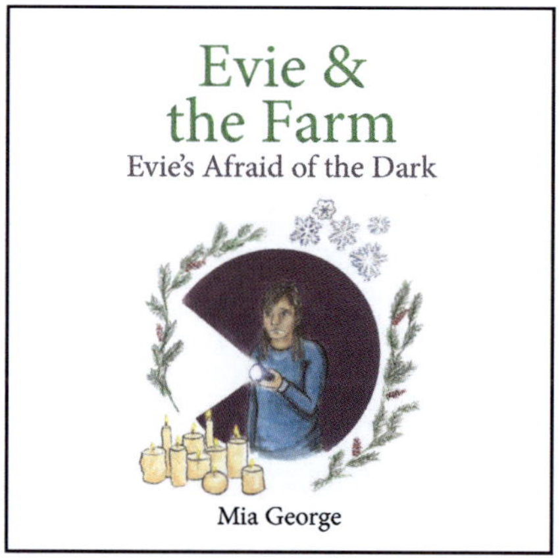

ISBN 978-1-7393812-0-2

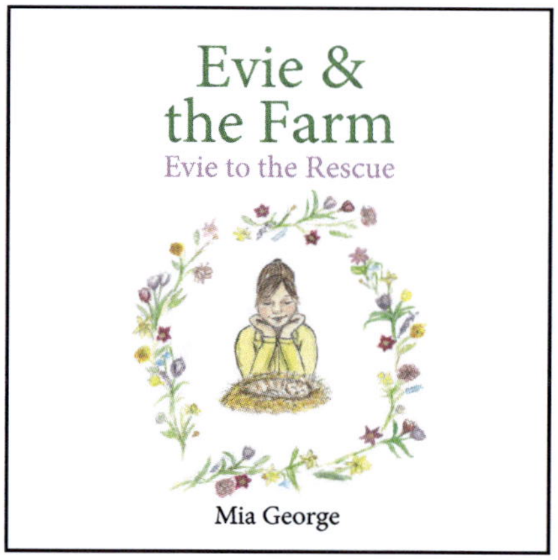

ISBN 978-1-7393812-1-9

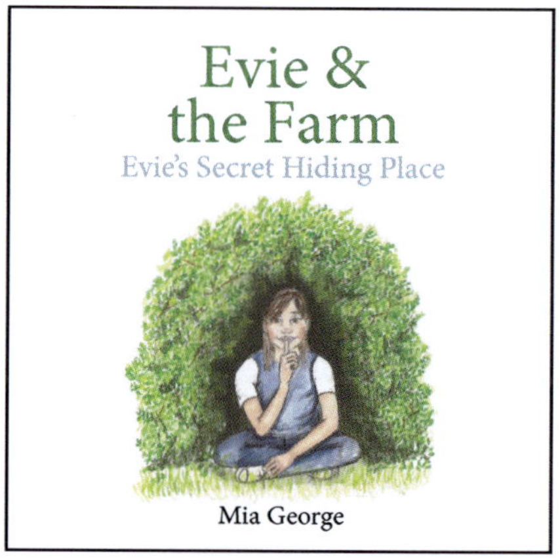

ISBN 978-1-7393812-2-6

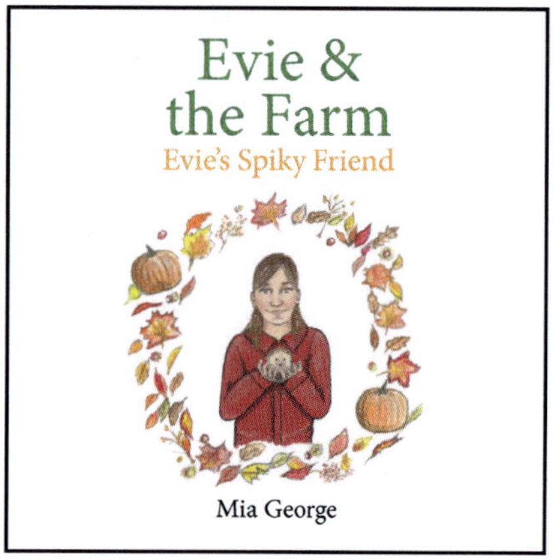

ISBN 978-1-7393812-3-3

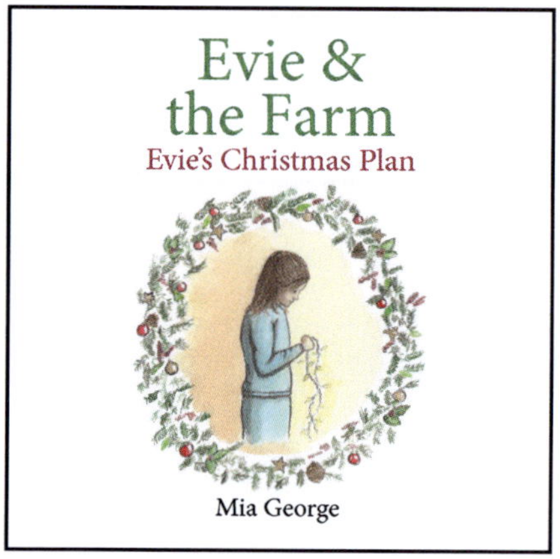

ISBN 978-1-7393812-4-0

Printed in Great Britain
by Amazon

22840475R00018